THe GuiTAR

2.9c

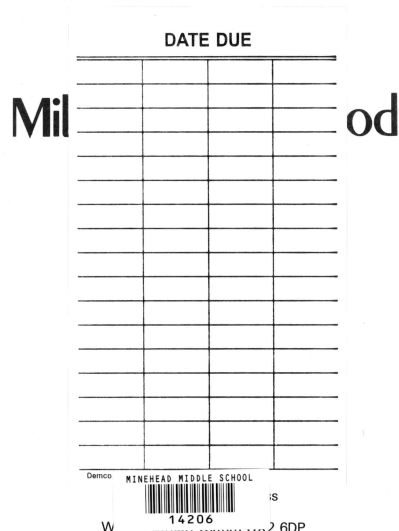

DATE DUE

Mil od

Demco

W alton Street, Oxford OX2 6DP

CONTENTS

Introduction

You will have seen the guitar played by performers in pop groups on television or perhaps at concerts, and you will know that groups use different sizes and shapes of guitar.

In this book you can read about the guitar now, how it is made and how it began. We tell you who played it—angels (in pictures), slaves, royalty, students, lovers serenading their loved ones, and famous composers as well as famous performers. At one time the guitar was despised because it was played by peasants, but later it came to be highly regarded again and was used all over the world. We tell you where it was played—in streets, in pubs, in palaces, in concert-halls, in drawing-rooms and in recording studios as well as on radio and television. We show how beautifully it can be made and decorated and how it appealed to painters.

We hope you enjoy the pictures as well as the stories, the information, the history and the questions about people you've heard of and people you haven't heard of yet. We hope you will find it interesting enough to go further, to find out more, to learn to play, and if you play already we hope it will inspire you to practise (every day)! And to play with other players . . .

(Opposite) Detail from a medieval painting showing angels playing mandora (an ancestor of the mandolin) and tambourine

String Instruments

The guitar is a string instrument. There are three separate families of string instruments, grouped according to the way they make their sound.

Plucked and bowed

The first family has as many notes as it has strings. When it is plucked each string sounds one note only. The harp and medieval psaltery work like this.

The instruments in the second family (violin, viola, 'cello and double bass) have only a few strings. Each string can be made to produce different notes when it is **stopped** (shortened, by being pressed down against a fingerboard). The player stops the strings with his or her left hand and makes them sound by playing with a bow in his right hand or plucking with his fingers (*pizzicato*).

▲ A Roman lady learning to play a plucked string instrument

▲ An Egyptian wall-painting showing early fretted instruments

Fretted instruments

The third family has strings which likewise are stopped by one hand and plucked by the other. Sometimes, however, you pluck with your fingers and sometimes with a small, hard object called a **plectrum,** which can be made of tortoiseshell, whalebone, ivory or bamboo. The guitar belongs to this family, which is called the **fretted** family because its members have **frets** or raised marks on the fingerboard underneath the strings to help the player to know where to press down the strings. Fretted instruments were known in ancient Egypt, China, Japan, India, Iceland, Greece, Persia and Europe, as well as Africa.

The Lute

The guitar is just one of several fretted instruments, of which perhaps the next best known is the **lute**. This instrument, which is shaped like half a pear, came from Arabia to Europe at about the time of the Crusades. Although there was a form of small lute in the 11th century called the **mandora**, which Italian medieval painters liked to show being played by angels, the lute was most popular during the 16th and 17th centuries. At this time lots of people composed music for the lute, including J.S. Bach. Many slender strips of wood (less than 1mm thick) were used to make the back of the instrument. This made delicate curved lutes so fragile that few of the older ones have survived till today.

The people who made lutes were called **luthiers**, a name used for makers of classical guitars too.

Shakespeare, the great English playwright who lived from 1564 to 1616, wrote a play about a bad-tempered girl (a 'shrew') called Katharine. She lost her temper with her music teacher and smashed her lute over his head. He comes on stage with the main body of the lute around his neck, but as Shakespeare sensibly directed her to smash it off-stage, the actors were able to use the same broken lute at each performance!

Here is a picture of a **bass lute,** or theorbo. It has two sets of strings. One set is fretted (see page 4), while the other set is played without being stopped (see page 4). It took a long time to get all the strings in tune. The strings were used in pairs, with each pair being tuned to the same note and played together to give a stronger sound. As the lute developed it was given more and more strings, and this made it so hard to play that people soon turned to easier instruments. The extra strings, you could say, strangled the instrument to death!

▼Playing the theorbo, or bass lute

▲ Louis XIV, with lute, and court musicians

Kings and titled people employed court lutenists to play the lute to them. John Dowland was an English lutenist who worked at the court of Queen Elizabeth I and at other European courts. As well as singing and playing he was also a composer and artists like Julian Bream (see page 35), who plays the lute as well as the guitar, perform a lot of his music. King Louis XIV, who ruled France from 1643 to 1715, had a court lutenist named Robert de Visée. He played and wrote music for both the lute and the guitar. In fact King Louis liked the guitar so much that he even learned to play it himself.

King Charles II of England (who reigned after Cromwell had died) spent a lot of time in France after his father Charles I was executed, and he learned the guitar too, from Louis's own teacher. When kings played instruments they obviously became fashionable. Even so, not everyone liked the guitar as much as Charles or Louis. One writer of the time, Samuel Pepys (pronounced 'peeps') the famous diarist, wrote:

> 'I heard a Frenchman play upon the guitar most extreme well, though at best methinks it is but a bawble (a cheap toy).'

The Mandolin

The **mandolin,** which is really a small lute, came from Italy in the 18th century. It had four or five *pairs* of strings. (As on larger lutes, a pair of strings, tuned to the same note, made a stronger sound than just one string.) As you can see in the picture, mandolins are beautifully made and decorated.

Beethoven (1770-1827) had a friend in Vienna, called Krumholz, who played the mandolin. Like other famous composers who wrote for this instrument (including Handel, Mozart, Stravinsky and Verdi) Beethoven wrote five pieces for mandolin and piano for his friend to play.

An Italian lady tuning her mandolin. Notice the pairs of strings ▼

The Vihuela

The **vihuela** was a Spanish instrument which was played by aristocrats and wealthy people. It was shaped more like a guitar than a lute, and it had a flat back. The instrument had more strings than the guitar, and could be played with a plectrum (like the guitar and mandolin) or plucked by the fingers (like the lute). Although peasants, students, gypsies and townspeople preferred the guitar to the lute, the rich Spanish preferred the vihuela, which flourished from the 14th to the 16th centuries.

The Cittern

The cittern was often called 'the English guitar', because the English liked it and played it from Tudor times right through to the 19th century, when Sor's concerts (see page 39) finally made the guitar more popular. The cittern had *wire* strings, tuned in pairs so that eight strings were tuned to four notes. It was played either by the fingers or with a plectrum.

So many people could play the cittern in London in Shakespeare's time that barbers kept one hanging on the wall of their shops.

They expected their customers to play, to amuse themselves as they waited their turn. Chaucer, an Englishman who wrote poetry 200 years earlier than Shakespeare (he lived from 1345-1400), tells us about the cittern also being kept in inns and taverns by landlords for their customers to use.

▲ An instrument-maker's workshop in 1751. How many different instruments can you name?

Questions

1 Describe the lute.
2 Explain why very few original lutes have survived.
3 Why did the lute become less popular as it developed?
4 What is the connection between royalty and the lute?
5 What is the connection between Beethoven and the mandolin?
6 What was the vihuela, and what type of people played it most?
7 Which instruments can or could be played with a plectrum?
8 What was the cittern's nick-name, and how did it get this?
9 How many strings did the cittern have, and how were they tuned?
10 How do we know that the cittern was played by a lot of people?

PROJECTS

1 With the help of your teacher, or through your local library, obtain a copy of the combined record and book set *Instruments of the Middle Ages and Renaissance* by David Munrow (see page 48 for details of this). On pages 75-83 of the book you'll find pictures of, and information about, all the instruments mentioned in this chapter except the mandolin. You can hear what the instruments sound like on side 4 (bands 6-14) of the record set. Put together an illustrated folder of information on the different instruments, perhaps including a reference to the mandora as the ancestor of the mandolin. Discuss with your friends the different sounds the instruments make.

2 Queen Elizabeth I was fond of the lute and particularly enjoyed listening to songs accompanied by this instrument. Here is part of a lute-song which was performed at her court. You can play the melody (Music **A**) on recorders, melodicas, or any other instruments that are available.

Once you've practised the tune divide into groups so that some of you can add the accompaniment (Music **B**). Guitarists can play the chords shown above the melody (see page 46 for fingering).

3 The following composers all wrote music for the mandolin: Handel, Mahler, Mozart, Schoenberg, Stravinsky, Verdi and Vivaldi. Use a music reference book to find out when each of these composers lived, and then write out their names in chronological order (this means putting in the order in which they were born). Next to their name write down three or more of the names of their compositions.

4 In this section two English writers, Shakespeare and Chaucer, have been mentioned. Look back to find out the connection between them and the guitar's relations, and then design your own chart which explains this connection.

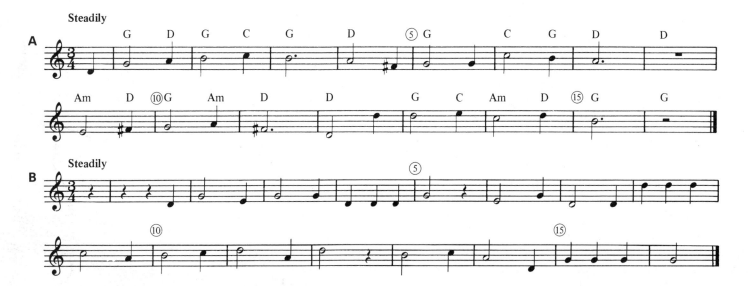

2 How The Guitar Is Made

And How It Works

The Classical Guitar

In the 17th and 18th centuries there were many guitar makers in France. They were called **luthiers**, the name also given to lute makers (see page 5). In Lyons a man called Lejeune had to go to jail because he made guitars which were copies of those made by someone called Duiffoprugcar. He not only copied the instrument, but also its special mark (like a trade mark), which is why he was sued by the original maker.

Ivory, ebony, mother-of-pearl and tortoise-shell were used to decorate these early guitars, and the strips of decoration round the edge were called **purfling**. This strengthened the edge as well as decorating it. Some instruments had decoration round the sound-hole too, and others had decorated backs.

Early guitars had four or five strings, but by the end of the 18th century the guitar had settled down to having six strings, though its size was not yet standard. You can see from the different

▲ A beautifully decorated 17th-century guitar

paintings (on page 47) that there were all sorts of shapes and designs.

The man who standardized the classical guitar was Antonio Torres, a Spaniard born in 1817, who died in 1892. By the 19th century a traveller complained that everyone in Spain had a guitar and played it at all hours of the day and night. Many guitar makers, or luthiers, were to be found in Spain therefore by this time.

Torres established the measurements of the classical guitar as follows:

Key to chapter opening (page 9)

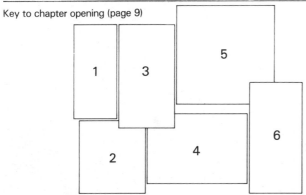

Making an acoustic guitar

1 Timbers waiting to be used: spruce (the light wood) for the top of the guitar rosewood (darker) for the body
2 Tapping and flexing a partly finished top
3 Shaping the side of a guitar on a bending iron
4 Getting ready to fit the rosette over the sound-hole
5 Gluing the back to the sides
6 Marking the position of the frets

▲ Purfling on a guitar made in 1641

The tone-quality of the classical guitar, which is very important, depends on the wood that it is made with. The top must be very thin (just over 1.5mm) so that it can vibrate well, but it must also be strong enough to stand up to the tension of the six guitar strings.

Torres developed an old idea from roof-building in cathedrals (called **fan-vaulting**) to make his guitar tops strong. You can see

from the picture that the wooden supporting strips, arranged in a fan shape, add strength and also help the vibration.

Spruce or pine is the best kind of wood for the top of the guitar, while for the body rosewood, mahogany or walnut is used. The wood needs to mature for a long time, shrinking and swelling with changing temperatures and humidity, so that it settles before it is used.

The strings of the guitar were once made of **gut,** but these tend to stretch and often need re-tuning. So the guitarist Segovia (see page 33) asked string makers to experiment with **nylon** which is firmer. As a result, the highest three strings today are made of gut or nylon, while the lower three are made of nylon wrapped round with copper wire, plated with bronze, silver or even gold. **Tuning machines** of ivory are used to adjust the tension of the strings. (NB: Never put steel strings on a classical guitar. The tension will be too strong for its delicate frame, and it will warp or break.)

THE FLAMENCO GUITAR

This originally came from Andalusia, Spain, and was used to provide rhythmic accompaniment to flamenco dancing and singing. Now it is built and played all over the world, for example in Japan and the U.S.A., and has been made popular by such artists as Paco de Lucia and Paco Peña. It weighs less than the classical guitar, and is held more in an upright position. **Pegs** of ebony, instead of tuning machines are used to wind the strings.

The flamenco guitar also has a more brilliant tone than the classical guitar, because it has a back and sides made of cypress, a neck of cedar and a fingerboard of ebony. The top has a plate of celluloid to protect it against the rhythmic taps of the player, who uses it almost like a drum. Flamenco guitar playing makes much use of the **rasgueado** technique, a downward stroke with the thumb or the backs of the finger nails which gives a very exciting sound. (See page 45.)

THE ACOUSTIC GUITAR

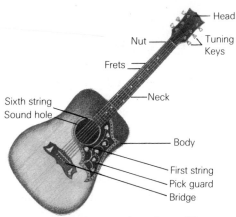

Head
Nut
Tuning Keys
Frets
Neck
Sixth string
Sound hole
Body
First string
Pick guard
Bridge

Guitars which are not electric are called **acoustic** guitars. The classical and flamenco guitars are in fact acoustic instruments, but as they were used a long time before electric guitars were invented, they keep their original names. When we speak of an acoustic guitar now we usually mean a steel-string guitar—the type used by folk singers and in dance bands.

The **steel-string guitar** is just over 11cm deep, 35.5cm wide (at its widest part) with a body of just over 48cm and an overall length of nearly one metre. There is also a jumbo version, which is the same depth, 5cm wider and longer, with a body just over 2cm longer. This extra size helps the sound to carry further. The body is made of rosewood, maple or mahogany, and the top is made of spruce or sometimes cedar.

The **arch-top** guitar used to be popular in the days of the 'big band' sound of the 1930s and '40s. It has two F shaped sound-holes (rather like those of a violin) instead of the large central sound hole of most other guitars. This guitar had heavy gauge strings and was used for the rhythm work in a dance band. There are now electric versions which jazz groups use.

The **twelve-string** guitar was used by some Blues singers (such as Huddie Ledbetter, better known as 'Leadbelly') and by many folk singers, including Pete Seeger. This guitar is still popular, and the twelve strings give a rich, throbbing sound to the backing chords.

THE ELECTRIC GUITAR

Folk singers and guitar players get a wide variety of tone-quality, whatever their music demands, by the way they use their hands, fingers, thumbs and nails. But electric guitars give different sounds according to how the controls of the instrument and its equipment are set: it is rather like the difference between the piano (which depends for its tone on the way the player's hands treat the keys) and the organ (which gives the tone the player wants by pressing or pulling the correct stops.)

▲ Two Gibson electric guitars: (left) solid-body and (right) arch-top electric acoustic model

On an electric guitar the vibrations of the strings are turned into electrical impulses by the guitar's pick-up. These impulses are then amplified and fed through a loudspeaker. Orville Gibson (1856 -1918) and Leo Fender (who was working until the 1960s) developed the first electric guitars, which is why so many modern instruments bear their names.

The **solid-body** guitar is capable of the loudest sound. It is heavy to hold because the body of the instrument is a slab of wood, hollowed out to hold the electric equipment, with controls on the outside. It has a bright treble sound and is used by rock musicians.

The **hollow-body** electric guitar has its own resonance as well as amplification. It has a deeper, more mellow tone than the solid body, has F-shaped sound holes and is used particularly by jazz guitarists.

The **semi-solid body** guitar is half way between the two described above. Although it has a solid centre, it is hollow at the sides. It also has F-shaped sound holes, and is used by Blues and Rock guitarists.

The Bass Guitar

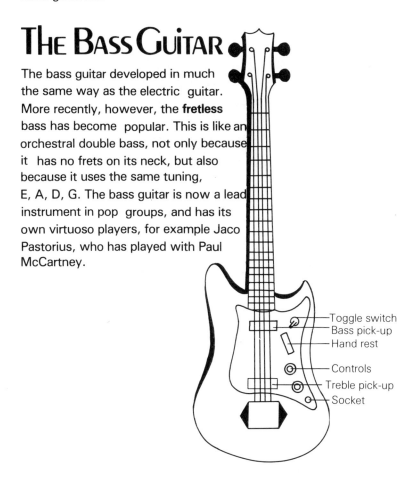

The bass guitar developed in much the same way as the electric guitar. More recently, however, the **fretless** bass has become popular. This is like an orchestral double bass, not only because it has no frets on its neck, but also because it uses the same tuning, E, A, D, G. The bass guitar is now a lead instrument in pop groups, and has its own virtuoso players, for example Jaco Pastorius, who has played with Paul McCartney.

Toggle switch
Bass pick-up
Hand rest
Controls
Treble pick-up
Socket

Amplification And Special Effects

As soon as the electric guitar's pick-up has turned the vibrations of the strings into electrical impulses, these impulses are then fed into a pre-amplifier, which has controls that the player can use to control what happens next to the sound. The impulses from the pre-amplifier are then fed into an amplifier and from there to the loudspeakers, so that the final sound can be heard by the player and the audience.

A good electric guitar amplifier has several special effects which can be used to alter the original sound of the guitar:

Tremolo This changes the volume of the sound from soft to loud and back to soft again very quickly. The speed of the tremolo can be altered, and a slow tremolo can give an echo effect.

Vibrato This changes the pitch of the guitar's sound, which means that the note 'wobbles' up and down.

Reverb Reverberation (its full name) is like a constant echo. It is the effect you get in a cave (or even in a bathroom!) when you call out. On a guitar, however, the amount of reverberation can be controlled and changed.

Fuzztone A fuzz-box, which can also be operated by a foot pedal, distorts the guitar's sound. It makes a whirring or fuzzing sound.

Echo Echo boxes produce their echo by using tape loops, with several playback heads close to each other. Recent echo machines use digital techniques based on microprocessors.

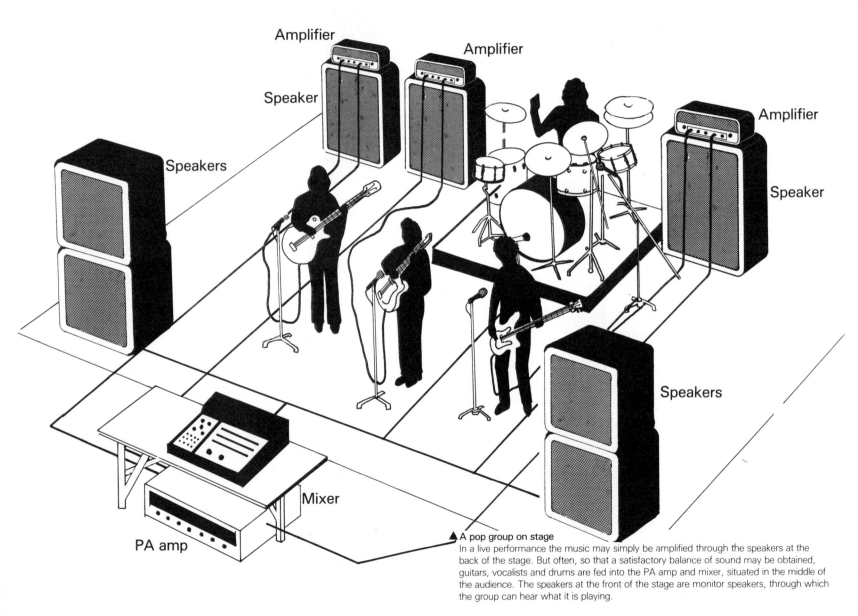

Amplifier

Amplifier

Amplifier

Speaker

Speakers

Speaker

Speakers

Mixer

PA amp

▲ A pop group on stage
In a live performance the music may simply be amplified through the speakers at the back of the stage. But often, so that a satisfactory balance of sound may be obtained, guitars, vocalists and drums are fed into the PA amp and mixer, situated in the middle of the audience. The speakers at the front of the stage are monitor speakers, through which the group can hear what it is playing.

Wah-wah This is the 'crying' effect produced by filtering the sound from the guitar, and changing the tone of the sound from very sharp to very dull to a regular rhythm. The effect is usually operated by a foot-pedal attachment to the amplifier.

QUESTIONS

1 What was a luthier?
2 Explain why a man called Lejeune went to jail in Lyons.
3 Explain what purfling was.
4 When did the guitar start to have six strings?
5 What are the body and strings of a guitar made of?
6 What are the differences between the classical and flamenco guitars?
7 Explain what an acoustic guitar is.
8 How does an electric guitar work?
9 What are the three different kinds of electric guitar, and how do they differ from each other?
10 What are some of the electric guitar's special effects?

PROJECTS

1 Here is part of a typical flamenco melody. It comes from the Granada region of Spain.
Play the melody on melodica or piano and notice the unusual interval marked [   ]. This interval is often used in eastern music and shows the eastern influences to be found in

▲ Rock musician with amplifier and wah-wah pedal

flamenco. Once you've learned the tune get a friend to join in, too. He or she can play this accompaniment on any instrument that's available:

Quite slowly

2 Make a list of all the records in the current top 20, and try to listen to them on one of the top 20 radio programmes. As you listen to each record, decide which, if any, of the special effects described on page 13 is used on each one. When you have done this, make a large chart to contain all this information. Which effects seem most popular? Try doing the same a few weeks later, when the charts have changed. What, if any, is the difference?

3 Folk Music Then And Now

Folk music is the kind that has been sung, played and made up by ordinary people for many hundreds of years. It was not written down because the people who made it and used it could not write music.

Although there has always been a lot of unaccompanied folk singing, the guitar and its relations have been among the most popular folk instruments, partly because the instrument is easy to carry, indoors or outdoors. The guitar can also be easily played while the guitarist sings.

Folk songs and folk dances vary according to their country of origin. Even England, Scotland and Wales have different types of music, as any songbook shows, but there is a special individual quality to music from the West Indies, Russia, Hungary, North Africa, Czechoslovakia, France, Austria, Germany and Spain.

The USA

Music from all these countries eventually found its way to America, as that huge land was taken over by people from Europe, Africa, South America and Mexico. When the Spaniards followed Columbus and invaded South America they established Spanish as the most-used language and the guitar as a useful instrument. People from this part of South America (especially Mexico) later moved North to the Western side of the States, and took their guitars with them.

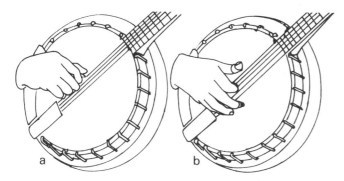

▲ a Strumming the banjo (with plectrum)
   b Finger-picking (with plectra on thumb, 1st and 2nd fingers)

The banjo

In North Africa a string instrument called the **banio** was used, and the slaves who came from this area were allowed to go on using it in the southern states of America, when the banio came to be called a **banjo**. In 1799 a white German musician who lived in Boston visited South Carolina. He heard slaves singing and playing the banjo, and enjoyed this so much that he bought their instrument, had a few lessons from them, and wrote a **minstrel song** which he published when he got back to Boston. This was the first black music published for white people to perform.

◀ (Opposite) Bob Dylan in concert

▼ Minstrel playing the banjo

Minstrels and cowboys

In 1843 the first regular minstrel troupe appeared on stage in America. They were so successful that they were followed by the **Kentucky Minstrels** and, most famous of all, the **Christy Minstrels.** The performers, who were white but played with blackened faces, sang to a banjo accompaniment, and then told jokes and funny stories. These shows became popular in England, and eventually on radio and television. There were hundreds of songs written especially for them. They tended to be funny or sentimental, and had the kind of chord-strumming, banjo-like accompaniment that was used in America to accompany the folk song.

Another specially American kind of music was that of the **cowboys.** Cowboys were expected to sing, to keep the cattle asleep at night and to keep themselves awake. The words of the songs cowhands used were made up as they went along, and were often about the places they were going to or coming from. But the tunes they used were well known folk tunes, and the guitar was the instrument they used to accompany their singing.

EUROPE

Many European composers in the 19th and 20th centuries discovered the appeal of folk music. For example, Chopin used the rhythm of the Polish peasants' dance, the **mazurka,** in his piano pieces; Grieg used the folk music of his native Norway in his piano music; and Vaughan Williams collected folk songs from English country areas and used some of them to make hymn tunes and other melodies in his own compositions.

Spain

In Russia, composers such as Rimsky-Korsakov and Balakirev not only used Russian folk music in their compositions, but were attracted by Spanish music too. Balakirev wrote *Overture on a Spanish Theme;* Rimsky-Korsakov wrote *Spanish Caprice* and Glinka wrote a piece called *Night in Madrid.* French composers

▲ Rimsky-Korsakov, a Russian composer influenced by Spanish folk music

also used Spanish folk music in their own compositions: Chabrier wrote a piece for orchestra, *España;* Debussy wrote *Ibéria,* and *La Soirée dans Grenade;* and Ravel wrote *Rapsodie espagnole.*

Spanish composers liked their own country's folk music too. Manuel de Falla (see page 40) organized a festival of folk song and dance in Granada in 1922, and used Spanish folk music to flavour his own compositions. Spain is especially rich in folk music. Flamenco is the name of the folk song and dance music of a part of Spain called Andalusia. Another area of Spain that has its own particular style is Catalonia.

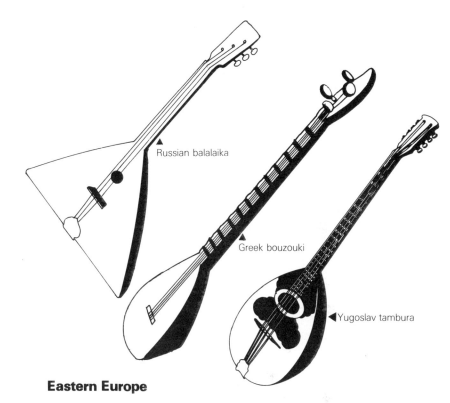

Russian balalaika

Greek bouzouki

◀Yugoslav tambura

Eastern Europe

In the 1920s there was a new interest in the folk songs and dances of Hungary and Romania. The famous composer Bela Bartók was born on the border between these two countries, and when he grew up he collected thousands of their work songs and folk dances. He then went to North Africa collecting songs, to try to find out about the connection between the two kinds. Zoltán Kodály, a friend of Bartók's, was another Hungarian composer who was very interested in folk music.

Gipsies or travelling people, are expert folk musicians. In Russia the gipsies used the **balalaika** as well as the guitar on which to play their folk music. Other relations of the guitar which have been used for folk music are the **bouzouki**, from Greece, and the **uti** and **tambura** from Yugoslavia. These instruments, however, have not become well known outside their own countries.

Modern Folk Music

Although folk music has been sung and played for many hundreds of years there is also a great deal of modern folk music. During the last twenty years there has been a revival of interest in folk music, with many folk clubs being formed throughout Britain where people can hear their favourite folk singers and performers. During the 1960s' Folk Revival some styles of folk-guitar playing became quite sophisticated, as you can hear if you listen to the music of Bert Jansch and John Renbourne.

Some folk musicians devised a method of tuning the strings of the guitar so that when all the strings were played open, they sounded a chord. This was called **open tuning,** e.g.

Normal tuning:	E	A	D	G	B	E
Open 'G':	D	G	D	G	B	D
Open 'C':	C	G	C	G	C	E

Open tuning was used frequently in the 'bottleneck blues' style (see page 24).

Although a lot of the music played at folk clubs is 'original' folk music, some folk singers make up their own folk songs, and often these are connected with something that is happening in the world today: **protest songs** are an example of this type of folk music. As with traditional folk music, the guitar is the most popular instrument used to accompany folk singing.

Protest music in the 20th century has been used to publicize certain issues (such as the hatred of war, or racial prejudice and equal rights for blacks) by writing simple catchy folk tunes about these subjects. These songs expressed the views of the people who sang them and often got more publicity for their cause.

The movement led by Dr Martin Luther King in America had two songs written for it which are still well known: *We shall overcome*

▼ Martin Luther King leading a freedom march in Detroit, USA

and *We shall not be moved.* Singing these songs kept up the spirits of protestors who often had to march many miles to make people aware of their ideas. Another well known protest song is *Where have all the flowers gone?,* an anti-war song which compares young men killed in war to the flowers of the nation.

Bob Dylan is perhaps the best known modern protest singer, although in recent years he has changed his style of singing several times. One of his best known songs is *Blowin' in the wind.* Like other modern folk singers he accompanies himself on the guitar. Another modern American folk singer is Pete Seeger, who once wrote and sang a folk song to try to save a park in Los Angeles from being built over. The Kingston Trio sang *A ship that never returned* in a campaign against the raising of subway fares in Boston.

Both Bob Dylan and Pete Seeger were influenced by an American folk singer who was a little older than them, Woody Guthrie. When a dust storm drove him away from the farm where he lived, he travelled around Oklahoma and California looking for work and singing to keep up his spirits and those of the people he was with. He learnt songs from his fellow-travellers and he wrote his own words to folk tunes, protesting about what he thought was wrong with the kind of life he and his fellow travellers had to live. The **talking blues**, a singing style used by black American preachers, appealed to Woody Guthrie. This is a way of speaking in rhythm over a sung accompaniment, or over a strummed guitar accompaniment.

QUESTIONS

1 What do we mean by folk music?
2 What is the connection between the guitar and folk music?
3 Explain how the music of Spain came to America.
4 What were minstrels?
5 How do you know that some Russian composers were influenced by the music of Spain?
6 Which Hungarian composers took a special interest in folk music?
7 What is protest music?
8 Give examples of 20th-century folk singers and some of their songs.
9 What do you know about Woody Guthrie?
10 What was talking blues?

PROJECTS

1 Cowboy songs (see page 18) are often accompanied by the guitar. Here's one from Texas called *The hell-bound train.* (The title is explained by the fact that the tune was originally sung by a cowboy who tells of a terrible nightmare that came to him after falling drunkenly asleep one night. During the nightmare he dreams he's aboard a train bound for hell. A train on which 'The imps for fuel are shovelling bones, and the furnace rings with a thousand groans'.)

Accompaniments

Play the tune on any instruments that you have, and add the accompaniments above once you've practised it. Guitarists, as usual, should play the chords as shown. Fingering for these can be found on page 46.

2 If you have any songbooks in school, try to look through one to see how many of the songs are folk songs: these will often say *traditional* or *anonymous* where the name of the song writer should appear. How many folk songs can you find? Look at the words of the folk songs in your book. What are the most popular subjects of folk songs? If you find out a lot of information (perhaps by looking at more than one songbook) you could make a chart to show what you have discovered.

3 Here's Bob Dylan's famous song *Mr tambourine man*. Play your version of it on recorders or melodicas. Guitarists can provide an accompaniment by playing the chords shown above it (see page 46 for fingering).

▲ Simon and Garfunkel: a song-writing and singing partnership with a distinctive modern folk style

4 Folk songs are songs written by ordinary folk, so why not try to make up a song yourself? You could use the tune of any simple folk songs you know or can find (your teacher will be able to help you here), and then make up some words of your own to go with it. Look at the words of other folk songs to give you some ideas of what you could write about—perhaps you feel strongly about something and could write a protest song (see page 20).

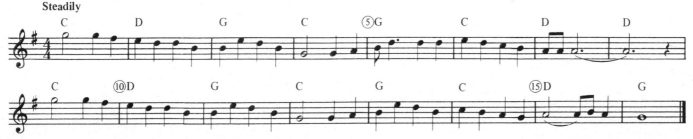

4 20th-Century Guitar Styles

In the 20th century the guitar has been the basic instrument for most popular music styles, especially those which are featured in this section of this book.

The Blues

▲ A Blues group broadcasting in the Southern States in the 1940s

The Blues, one of the first styles of black music, developed out of the sadness that was part of being a black American. During slavery, blacks had worked under the most wretched conditions, and the **work songs** and **field-hollers** that they made up were often sad and bitter.

The rhythms of the African music that the first slaves had brought to America were complex and its scales were also different from the scales of Western music since the Africans used extra notes in between our own. These notes found their way into Blue music, and are called **Blue notes.** They help to give Blues its distinctive and rather sad sound. Most Blues music follows a repeating twelve-bar sequence like the example on page 30.

Playing accompaniments for the Blues singer was often a problem. The guitar is a fretted instrument (see page 4) and the frets are arranged to make the notes of the European scale. However, the Blues singers needed the extra Blue notes, and one famous Blues singer, **Son House,** found out how to get them.

Son House heard a guitar player making the kind of sound he needed, and so he went to see how he got it. The player had a bottle neck on his left hand index fingers, and he used this to press down all the guitar strings at once, and then slide up or down the strings to get the notes and chords he needed in between the 'normal' guitar notes. When Son House tried to do the same thing he cut his finger several times, but the bottle neck still worked in the same way, and so this style of guitar playing became quite popular for playing the Blues. Later players used a metal slide instead, and this is commonly used today. (NB: Do not try to use a bottle neck on a guitar yourself, as this could be dangerous.)

Leadbelly (real name, Huddie Ledbetter, see page 25) was a Blues performer who used a twelve-string guitar (see page 12). Wes Montgomery was another great Blues player, who died at the early age of 45 in 1968, but who is considered a legend among those who heard him or who have his records.

As blacks were forced to move north into the cities in America, the Blues developed into a style that became known as **City Blues.** This was a rather harsher sounding Blues. When the first electric guitars came to be used in City Blues, saxophones were also added to the music, and gradually **Rhythm and Blues** developed in the 1940s. **Muddy Waters** and **Howlin' Wolf** are examples of early Rhythm and Blues performers.

In the 1960s there was a revival of Rhythm and Blues. Groups like **The Rolling Stones** based their style of modern pop music on 'R and B', as it came to be known by its fans.

▼Playing with a bottleneck

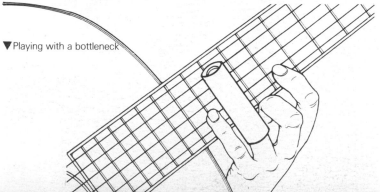

▲ Huddie Ledbetter, or 'Leadbelly'

▼ Bukka White playing with a bottleneck

▲ Muddy Waters, king of Rhythm and Blues

Rock 'n' Roll

The guitar was even more important to rock 'n' roll than it was to the Blues. By the time rock 'n' roll emerged in the early 1950s, the guitar was an essential part of any group. Although acoustic guitars were used at first by many performers, electric instruments soon became the norm, partly because they were able to make a louder sound.

Rock 'n' roll was really a mixture of two earlier styles of music: Rhythm and Blues (see page 24) and Country and Western. The electric guitar was used in Rhythm and Blues, but in Country and Western music the guitar was not so important; in fact the banjo was sometimes used in Country music, as well as the violin.

▼ Bill Haley and his Comets

▲ Skiffle group in 1957

One of the reasons that rock 'n' roll developed from these two other styles was that the first rock 'n' roll musicians, such as Bill Haley and Elvis Presley, were involved with both types of music in one way or another, and seemed to bring the two together. Bill Haley was originally a country singer, but when the Decca record company got Haley to record a Rhythm and Blues song, *Shake, Rattle and Roll,* it became an instant success. Elvis Presley grew up in Memphis, only 200 miles from Nashville, which was the centre of Country music. But he lived in a black ghetto, and must have heard a lot of Rhythm and Blues music. His first record, *That's Alright Mama* was a Blues song, but it had a Country song on the B side of the record.

Bill Haley and Elvis Presley both played the guitar. So did the early English rock 'n' roll singers, such as Tommy Steele and Cliff Richard, who started off their careers in the late 1950s by imitating the two Americans.

Skiffle

Skiffle was one style of music where only an acoustic guitar was used: in fact, all the instruments in a skiffle group were pretty simple, the others usually being a tea-chest bass and a washboard! Skiffle was a British style of music that appeared in the late 1950s. It was similar to American 'jugband' music, where very everyday words were put to a simple tune, and where often only three basic chords were used to accompany the singing. Skiffle was introduced into Britain by Lonnie Donegan, whose record *Rock Island Line* became a hit for him in 1956. Donegan also played the banjo as well as the acoustic guitar, and he later became famous for some humorous songs. *Does your chewing gum lose its flavour on the bedpost overnight?* and *My old man's a dustman* (which got to Number 1 in the British Charts in 1960) were both hits for him.

The 1960s

▲ The Shadows with Hank Marvin (far right) on lead guitar

The 1960s were a busy ten years for pop music, and for the development of the guitar in pop. In the 1950s the guitar had really been used as an *accompanying* instrument, usually playing chords while a singer sang the tune. Although electric instruments began to be used during this time, the guitar didn't stand out from other instruments, and rarely had a solo part, even though it was considered an essential rock 'n' roll instrument.

In the 1960s however, pop music developed considerably, and so did the parts that guitars had to play. Cliff Richard's backing group, **The Shadows,** got to number 1 in the top 20 charts with their guitar instrumental *Apache* in 1960, and had several further successes with purely instrumental records after that. By this time the **bass guitar** (see page 13) was established as an alternative to the old string bass, or double bass, which was used in the very early days of rock 'n' roll, for example by Bill Haley's backing group, **The Comets.**

The most important group of the 1960s was **The Beatles,** who from 1963, with their first number 1 hit, *She loves you,* continued to be the most successful pop musicians until their break-up at the end of the decade. One of the reasons for their continued success was the fact that they *developed* their music, and made it more interesting musically: this meant that the guitar parts in their songs also became more interesting.

The Beatles' early hits, such as *She loves you* and *I wanna hold your hand,* had very simple guitar accompaniments; other later songs, such as *Eleanor Rigby,* had different instruments, while songs such as *Yesterday* had a simple acoustic guitar accompaniment. But some of the later tracks of LPs, such as those on *Sergeant Pepper's lonely hearts' club band* in 1967, became more demanding for the players. Later still, the Beatles were influenced by Indian music, and used the Indian version of the guitar, the **sitar,** in their music.

▼ The Rolling Stones: along with the Beatles they were one of the most important groups of the 1960s

The Rolling Stones (see page 27) were almost as popular as The Beatles at about the same time, and managed to be successful partly because they were so different from The Beatles in their music and their manner. The Stones were much more aggressive when performing with Mick Jagger, their lead singer, who became well known for his unusual and exciting dancing when he was singing. The Stones music was heavily based on Rhythm and Blues (see page 24), and in songs like *Satisfaction,* which reached number 1 in 1965, the guitar parts are loud and forceful.

But British groups were not the only ones to develop the importance of the guitar in the 1960s. One American vocal group which had its own very distinctive sound was **The Beach Boys.** Their record, *Good Vibrations,* which reached number 1 in Britain and the USA in 1966, gave the bass guitar a more interesting part in the opening than the instrument usually got at that time.

THE LATE 1960S AND BEYOND

▲ Pete Townsend (of The Who) performing guitar acrobatics

By the late 1960s pop music had developed a great deal. Guitar playing for some groups had become very aggressive, and **The Who** even went as far as smashing their guitars against amplifiers as a gimmick!

The most important development for the guitar, however, was the emergence of the *virtuoso* performer. Jimi Hendrix has been described as the greatest guitar player in the history of pop. He was half negro and half Mexican, born in Seattle, Washington. Like several other pop musicians he died of a drug overdose. Eric Clapton helped form a group called **The Cream** in 1967, which consisted only of virtuoso players. Clapton was the guitarist, and has made several successful LPs since that time.

Another successful and very able guitar player of this time was Jimmy Page, who in 1968 formed **Led Zeppelin**. This group was not very well known considering how very successful it was: four of its first five LPs got to number 1 in the LP top 10, while one of them stayed in the top 10 for over a year!

Black music began to develop more by the late 1960s, with the arrival of Soul music in Britain from America. The instrumental side of this music was less important than the enthusiastic singing, and so most Soul records did not give the guitar a lot to do. A very popular form of black music in the 1970s was Reggae, in which the guitar backing played on the 'off-beat' for most of the time.

QUESTIONS

1 How did the music of negro slaves differ from Western music?
2 What unusual style of guitar playing did Son House develop?
3 What new style of Blues developed as blacks were forced to move into the northern cities of America?
4 Why did electric guitars soon become popular with rock 'n' roll groups?
5 Which four rock 'n' roll singers also played the guitar?
6 What songs made Lonnie Donegan famous?
7 How did the use of the guitar in pop music change in the 1960s?
8 What kind of guitar playing did the Beatles and Rolling Stones develop?
9 What was unusual about the guitar playing of The Who?
10 Name some virtuoso guitar players of the 1960s.

The Third World Reggae band ▶

Projects

1 Here is a simple blues accompaniment. Read through the chapter on *Teach yourself the guitar* (if you are new to the instrument) and try it out with a friend playing the piano part. Fit it to a song you know, or make one up yourself.

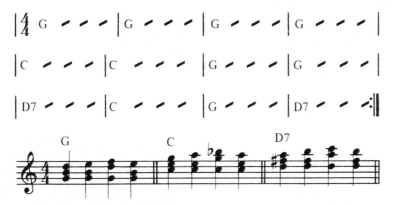

2 Jimi Hendrix (see page 28) composed a song called *Voodoo chile* which is mostly based on one chord. A version of the song appears on his 1968 *Electric Ladyland* album during which Hendrix and the other members of his band, The Experience, each take turns making up new melodies to go with the basic chord. This process of making things up on the spot is called **extemporization.** And listening to the exciting extemporizations of The Jimi Hendrix Experience in *Voodoo chile* you'd never guess that all the musicians had to go on was one chord. Here are just two of the tunes played by the bass guitarist on the recording:

1. **Easily**

2. **Easily**

Try them out on any instruments that are available (the lower pitched the better). Then repeat each of them many times, getting some members of the group to play the basic chord on guitars and piano. Then take turns at making up tunes to fit with the bass part and chord.

3 This section has tried to show how guitar music has developed since pop music began this century. EITHER write your own 'history of pop guitar music', using this information plus any other facts you can find; OR, make a poster for your classroom wall on the same subject.

4 If you are able to get hold of any of the records mentioned in this section (your parents or their friends may have some), listen to them. If possible, try to listen to one from each of the periods of time mentioned, and try to compare the guitar parts in each. Can you hear how the guitar developed during the 1960s?

Key to opposite page

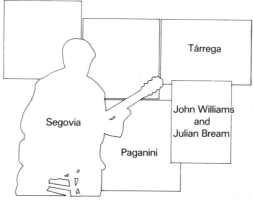

JULIAN BREAM
Villa-Lobos
The
Twelve Etudes for Guitar
Suite populaire brésilienne

RCA
RED SEAL

"Guitarist par excellence" New York Herald Tribune   TWO FAVORITE GUITAR CONCERTOS
JOHN WILLIAMS / EUGENE ORMANDY
RODRIGO/Concierto de Aranjuez   CASTELNUOVO-TEDESCO/Concerto in D
MEMBERS OF THE PHILADELPHIA ORCHESTRA

This section is about famous guitar players from the past. Although some of the performers mentioned were also composers for the instrument too (such as Paganini), they were more famous for their playing than for anything else.

Paganini

Niccolò Paganini was born in Genoa, Italy, in 1782 and died in 1840. His family was very poor, but he became a brilliant violinist, and was already famous in Italy when he visited Vienna, Paris and London from 1828 to 1832. He retired, rich, in 1834.

Paganini played the guitar as brilliantly as he played the violin, and he composed music as well for both these instruments. When he performed his duets for guitar and violin it was he who played the guitar part, while he got a friend to play the violin part. He wrote 12 **sonatas** (pieces with several contrasting sections) for violin and guitar.

It is difficult to play some of Paganini's works now, as he only wrote in full what the *other* player had to perform. He kept his own part secret, never writing it out properly, so that no one else could practise it and try to play as well as he did.

Audiences were so excited by Paganini's playing that they would touch him in the street after his concerts, to find out if he was real. Famous composers, such as Schubert, Chopin and Liszt, wrote with amazement about how well he played, and some composers borrowed some of his melodies and wrote variations on them: Schumann, Liszt, Brahms and Rachmaninov paid him this compliment. To excite his audiences and to show off, Paganini would sometimes play blindfold, cut off some of the strings of his instrument, and just play on the few that were left!

Tárrega

Francisco Tárrega was born in Spain in 1852 and died in 1909. Like Paganini's, his family was poor, but he was still able to learn to play both the piano and the guitar. He decided to concentrate on the guitar, and eventually became a famous teacher.

In those days the guitar was used mainly to accompany singing and dancing, but Tárrega enlarged its **repertoire** (the pieces written for it) by re-writing piano pieces by Beethoven, Chopin, and Schumann for the guitar. He also wrote studies and pieces for it himself. Albéniz (1860-1909), the famous piano composer, thought that many of his own pieces sounded just as good when Tárrega played them on the guitar.

Tárrega used to practise for three or four hours every day. He spent time on scales, arpeggios (chords played one note at a time very quickly), trills, runs, and used a watch to make sure that he spent enough time on each of these. He hated giving concerts, and although he did come to England once to play, he did not like the cold, or the fog, and not being able to understand the language.

Tárrega introduced new ways of playing the guitar. Until his time one of the most common strokes had been a downward strum with the thumb or nails called **rasgueado** (see page 11). Tárrega introduced a stroke called **apoyando,** where the finger is pushed across the string, coming to rest on the string below.

Segovia

The classical guitar owes its popularity today to one man—Andrés Segovia, who was born in Spain in 1893. When he wished to learn the guitar his family hated the idea. The guitar, they argued, was played by peasants and gipsies, in taverns and in the streets. It was not a way of becoming a 'proper' musician or of earning a living.

Since his family would not let him have lessons, Segovia had to teach himself. He was a natural musician and taught himself so well that he could soon teach others, even though *he* had never had a lesson. He did not own a good concert guitar until 1916, the year he played his first public concert in Madrid. He played the music of Sor (see page 39) and of Tárrega (see page 32), and music that J.S. Bach had originally written for the lute. He also found and republished old music such as that by Visée (see page 6). Even so, there was still little music for the classical guitar, and so Segovia followed Tárrega's example, and made guitar arrangements of other composers' music originally intended for other instruments.

By the time Segovia played his first concert in Paris, in 1924, his fame had spread, and a composer called Roussel gave him a new piece for solo guitar which was simply entitled *Segovia.* Many modern composers wrote pieces especially for him. They realized from his playing how interesting the guitar could sound, and how many varieties of tone it had in the hands of an expert.

In 1928 Segovia played in New York, and later toured Japan, China and the Philippines. Then came concerts in Europe and in South America. He could always fill the largest of concert halls with people, and with his sound. Most of the people discussed in the rest of this section first became involved with the guitar because of their delight at the way Segovia played it—some were even taught by him.

▲ The artist Jean Cocteau's view of jazz guitarist Django Reinhardt

Django Reinhardt

Django Reinhardt was a French gipsy who was born in Belgium in 1910. Music has always played an important part in the life of gipsies, and so from an early age Django was brought up among music. He never went to school, had no lessons, could write nothing except his name, and certainly could not read or write music.

Django wanted a guitar when he was very young, and when he did get one (not until he was 12!) he listened to the gipsy players, watched them, copied them and eventually taught himself to play. Obviously he had the talent to become a great jazz guitarist and would let nothing stand in his way. When he was 18, two fingers of his left hand were badly damaged when a caravan set on fire, but in spite of this he continued to practise the guitar until he could play brilliantly.

Django will probably be best remembered for founding the famous quintet of the **Hot-Club de France.** This was a group of five jazz players: three guitars, a violin and a bass. He visited America after the second world war and became as famous in America as he was in Europe. Although he arranged and composed a lot of music for jazz groups, this was not written down and was later forgotten. The only music of his that we now know is that which he recorded.

Django enjoyed all kinds of music, including that of Bach and Berlioz, but couldn't play any of this since he couldn't read music. Instead, he went to hear it at concerts. He believed (and you may well think he was right!) that people who put barriers between one kind of music and another, and who shut whole areas of music out of their lives, are silly.

▲Django was much influenced by gipsy music

Julian Bream

Julian Bream was born in London in 1933, and has played all over the world, made records, appeared on television, and taught on both sides of the Atlantic. As well as the guitar he plays the lute, both as a solo instrument and with a group of people who play other 16th-and 17th-century instruments. He also plays jazz guitar with friends.

The composer **Malcolm Arnold** (born in 1921) has written tuneful music for Bream, including a guitar concerto and a piece called *Elegy for Django Reinhardt* (see page 34). Benjamin Britten (1913-1976) wrote *Songs from the Chinese* for the tenor Peter Pears to perform with the guitar accompaniment played by Julian Bream. In 1964 Britten wrote a piece which was very adventurous called *Nocturnal* and which used a theme by the Elizabethan composer John Dowland. Bream tells how he went out to lunch with Britten when this piece was being written.

'Is it possible to play this chord, like this, on the guitar?', asked the composer. Bream stretched his fingers over an imaginary guitar, trying several fingerings, and finally said 'No'. They finished the meal, and as they parted Britten said 'Keep trying'. Challenged like this Bream did keep trying, and after much thought he found a way to stretch his hand over the awkward chord and phoned the composer to say that although it was very difficult it was not *quite* impossible.

▲ John Williams (left) and Julian Bream

◀ The composer Benjamin Britten who had a long association with Bream and wrote guitar music for him

John Williams

John Williams was born in Australia in 1946. His father began to teach him the guitar when he was six, when the family moved to London where John's father opened the Spanish Guitar Centre. The classical guitar was being taken very seriously by composers, and although many people wished to learn to play like Segovia, there was a shortage of good teachers. At that time there was no professor of guitar at either the Royal College of Music or the Royal Academy of Music.

So John Williams went to Italy to study under Segovia himself. He was such a successful student that at the age of nineteen he was made professor of guitar at the Royal College of Music. Like Julian Bream (see page 35) he plays all over the world, makes records, plays on television and has music specially written for him by other composers. He has also been involved in playing jazz and rock guitar, and his group **Sky** attract large audiences at their concerts.

Questions

1 How did Paganini make sure that no one would play his own compsitions as well as he did?
2 What effect did Paganini have on audiences and on other composers?
3 How did Tárrega enlarge the guitar's repertoire?
4 What new method of playing the guitar did Tárrega develop?
5 How did Segovia learn the guitar, and what difficulties did he face?
6 What kind of music did Segovia play, and how did he add to the repertoire of the classical guitar?
7 Which composers have written music especially for Julian Bream?
8 What story tells you that Julian Bream would not allow a difficult piece of guitar music to defeat him?
9 Why did John Williams have to go to Italy to study the guitar?
10 What post did John Williams hold at an unusually early age?

Projects

1 Paganini wrote a tune which several composers have added variations to (see page 32). Try to listen to two very different but enjoyable examples, Rachmaninov's *Variations on a Theme of Paganini* and the LP simply called *Variations,* by Andrew Lloyd Webber. What do you notice about each piece, which do you prefer, and why? Write about each version.
2 How many of your school's records are of guitar music? Make a list of them, naming the pieces and the performers.
3 Borrow a record catalogue (an old one will do), and see how many pages there are of classical guitar recordings. How many records have Segovia, Bream and John Williams made?
4 On the *Sky 2* double album John Williams (see page 36) plays acoustic guitar in *Ballet-Volta* (side 3) and electric guitar during *Vivaldi* (side 4). Listen to these two tracks and then decide which instrument you prefer. Then think about the reasons for Williams's choice of instrument for each piece. (For details of the *Sky 2* album see page 48).

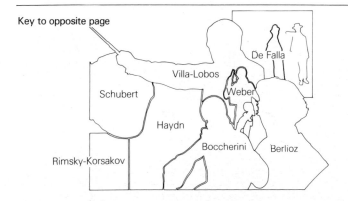

Key to opposite page

De Falla
Villa-Lobos
Schubert
Weber
Haydn
Rimsky-Korsakov
Boccherini
Berlioz

6 Some Guitar Composers

Here is some information about a selection of composers from the past, and recent past, who have been connected in some way with the guitar. Some of them you will have already heard of, though the guitar's most famous composers may well be unfamiliar.

HAydN

Franz Joseph **Haydn** was born in Austria in 1732, and died in its capital, Vienna, in 1809. He was chief musician to a Prince, and was famous on his master's country estate as a good shot and a good fisherman, as well as an excellent composer. Among his many compositions (including over 100 symphonies!) he wrote a **trio** (a piece for three instruments) for guitar, violin and cello.

King Ferdinand of Naples asked Haydn to write five concertos (pieces for a solo instrument and orchestra in several sections). This King played an odd instrument, a hand-cranked **hurdy-gurdy**. Although no-one else liked it, they had to put up with it since the King played it. Haydn wrote five concertos which pleased the King

so much that he ordered eight more. Haydn like the concertos too, and re-wrote them for more popular instruments, including the guitar. Number three, for two guitars and orchestra, is still played today.

BocchERiNi

Luigi **Boccherini** was born in Lucca, Italy, in 1743, and died in Madrid, Spain, in 1805. He got a job as a household composer to the King of Spain's brother. Boccherini played the cello and he didn't like either the guitar or Spanish music very much. However, he was asked to write some chamber music which used the guitar. He wrote twelve tuneful **quintets** (pieces for five instruments) for two violins, guitar, viola and cello. In the fourth one he used a Spanish folk dance, the fandango. Even though he didn't care for the guitar himself, Boccherini's quintets are some of the most enjoyable classical music ever written for this instrument.

SchubERt

Franz **Schubert** was born in Vienna in 1797 and died there in 1828. He played the guitar, as well as the piano and violin. He also sang in the choir of Vienna Cathedral, as Haydn had done many years earlier. (This choir is now known as the Vienna Boys' Choir.)

Schubert wrote over 600 songs, which is more than any other composer had done. He used to sing them in bed before getting up in the morning, accompanying himself on the guitar. We know this because it amused his friends, and one of them wrote about it. When Schubert had tried out the accompaniment on the guitar, he would write it down for the piano.

▲ Haydn and   a hurdy-gurdy player ▲

Weber And Berlioz

▲ Berlioz playing the guitar

Carl Maria von **Weber** was born in 1786 and died in London in 1826. (He stayed in London to conduct a performance of one of his own operas, and died of tuberculosis.) He was most famous for his operas, but he played the piano and the guitar very well. He wrote a **divertimento** (a piece intended to entertain, or 'divert' the listener) for piano and guitar. 90 of his songs are written with a guitar accompaniment, and are rarely performed now.

Hector **Berlioz** was born in the south of France in 1803 and died in Paris in 1869. His father was a doctor and sent Berlioz to Paris to study medicine. Young Berlioz didn't want to be a doctor so he studied music instead, but didn't dare to tell his father. He could play the guitar very well and when he couldn't earn his living as a composer he gave guitar lessons.

As a boy Berlioz listened while his sister had guitar lessons, and asked if he could learn the instrument as well. After the first lesson the teacher discovered that the pupil could already play better than the teacher. Berlioz tells us this himself, in his autobiography—though he is probably exaggerating! Despite his virtuosity as a performer, however, he never wrote anything for the guitar.

Sor

Fernando **Sor** was born in Barcelona, Spain, in 1778. He was becoming famous in Spain as a composer and guitar-player at the time of the Napoleonic wars. The French and some of the Spaniards fought the English and the rest of the Spaniards. Sor was an officer in the army that helped the French, and when they were defeated he left Spain for good.

Sor composed many ballets and married a French ballet-dancer. They both went to Russia, and she was so popular there as a ballet teacher that she stayed there. When Sor played in England he was a great success. The English forgot about the 'English guitar' or **cittern** (see page 7) that had been played for over 200 years: the Spanish guitar became popular instead, because everyone wanted to play like Sor.

For the guitar, Sor composed variations on themes by Mozart and Hummel, Spanish dances, a concertante for Spanish guitar and strings and a duet for two guitars called *The Two Friends.* (This was dedicated to a friend who played the guitar with him.)

Sor's most famous work was *Méthode pour la Guitare,* a handbook on how to play the guitar published in Paris in 1830.

Although it is perhaps the most important book on guitar-playing ever written, few living performers have the chance of seeing it, and have to be content with playing a few pieces from it. He also wrote some **studies** (pieces specially written to help the player practise something that is difficult to do), some 'easy exercises' and 'pieces for lessons'. All famous modern players of the classical guitar have studied his work. Sor died in 1839, at about the time the guitar was becoming popular with ordinary people.

▲De Falla (left) and the dancer-choreographer Massine for whom he wrote *The Three-Cornered Hat*

De Falla

Manuel de **Falla** was born in Cadiz, Spain, in 1876, and died in 1946. He was a famous Spanish composer and was interested in Spanish folk music (see page 19). He wrote music for a ballet, called *The Three-Cornered Hat,* three pieces for piano and orchestra called *Nights in the Gardens of Spain,* and one splendid guitar solo. This was a tribute to the French composer Debussy, with whom de Falla was friendly, and was called *Homage to Debussy*.

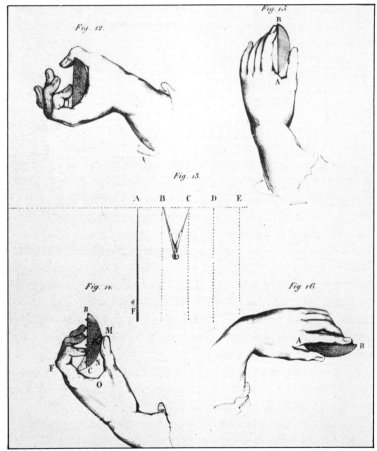

▲ A page from Sor's *Méthode pour la Guitare,* showing hand positions

Ponce And Villa-Lobos

Manuel **Ponce** was a Mexican, born in 1882, who died in 1948. Segovia (see page 33) spent a lot of time in Mexico and South America. In 1941, in Montevideo, Segovia gave the first performance of Manuel Ponce's concerto for guitar and orchestra. Ponce's *Sonata Romantica* is sub-titled 'Homage to Franz Schubert', who loved the guitar, while his *Sonata Classica* is sub-titled 'Homage to Fernando Sor'. Both these works are written in a way that reminds the listener of the music of Schubert and Sor, partly because Ponce studied the music of all the previous composers for this instrument. Ponce's other guitar music, for example *Twelve Preludes* and *Sonata III,* is more modern in style.

Heitor **Villa-Lobos** (1887-1959) was a Brazilian. He first met Segovia in 1924 and he borrowed the guitarist's instrument to try out some music. This worried the guitar's owner very much, as Villa-Lobos played it clumsily; but he wrote for it very well. He wrote *Twelve Studies* and *Five Preludes* for guitar, as well as a guitar concerto, and is considered one of the most important guitar composers.

Castelnuovo-Tedesco And Rodrigo

Joaquin **Rodrigo** (born 1902), a blind Spanish composer, has written many works for the guitar, including two of the most popular classical pieces composed this century: *Concierto de Aranjuez* (specially written for Segovia) and *Fantasia para un Gentilhombre.* Look for a record of the concerto: its slow movement was made into a hit record, and its fast movements are rhythmic and very lively.

Mario **Castelnuovo-Tedesco** (1895-1968) was Italian. (If you find Castelnuovo difficult to remember, just remember that it means Newcastle!) Like Ponce, he remembered past composers who had written for the guitar, and especially two Italian composers. His *Capriccio Diabolico* ('Devilish Caprice') is sub-titled 'Homage to Paganini', and his guitar sonata is sub-titled 'Homage to Boccherini'. (Perhaps he was also thinking of Boccherini when he wrote a quintet for guitar and strings in 1953.) Castelnuovo-Tedesco is best known for his *Concerto in D for guitar and orchestra* (specially composed for Segovia), one of the most famous works ever written for classical guitar.

▶The Brazilian composer Heitor Villa-Lobos

Questions

1 What is the connection between Haydn and the hurdy-gurdy?
2 Which guitar composer didn't actually like the instrument?
3 Explain how Schubert used to test the accompaniments to his songs.
4 What are the connections between Weber and the guitar?
5 How did Berlioz probably exaggerate his ability on the guitar?
6 Explain how Fernando Sor came to leave Spain.
7 What was *Homage to Debussy,* and how did it get its name?
8 What are the connections between Ponce, Segovia, Schubert and Sor?
9 Which two past guitar composers did Castelnuovo-Tedesco 'remember'?
10 Name two guitar compositions by Rodrigo.

Projects

1 Here is the melody (Music **A**) of a short piece by Sor (see page 39).
   Play the melody on recorders, melodicas, or any other instruments that are available. Then divide into groups so that some of you can play Sor's tune and the others the accompaniment (Music **B**).
   Guitarists can have a shot at playing the melody or put in the chords which are shown above it. (See page 46 for chord fingering.)
2 Listen to music composed by any of the people in this section. What do you think of it? Write a short report on any music that you hear.
3 Do you play an instrument? If so, could you write a handbook for it, just as Sor wrote his for the guitar (see page 40)? Write, design and produce the first page of such a book, and include diagrams, pictures and even some studies if you wish.

A

Quite fast

*D♯ in the original

B

Quite fast

Repeat from beginning to ⊕

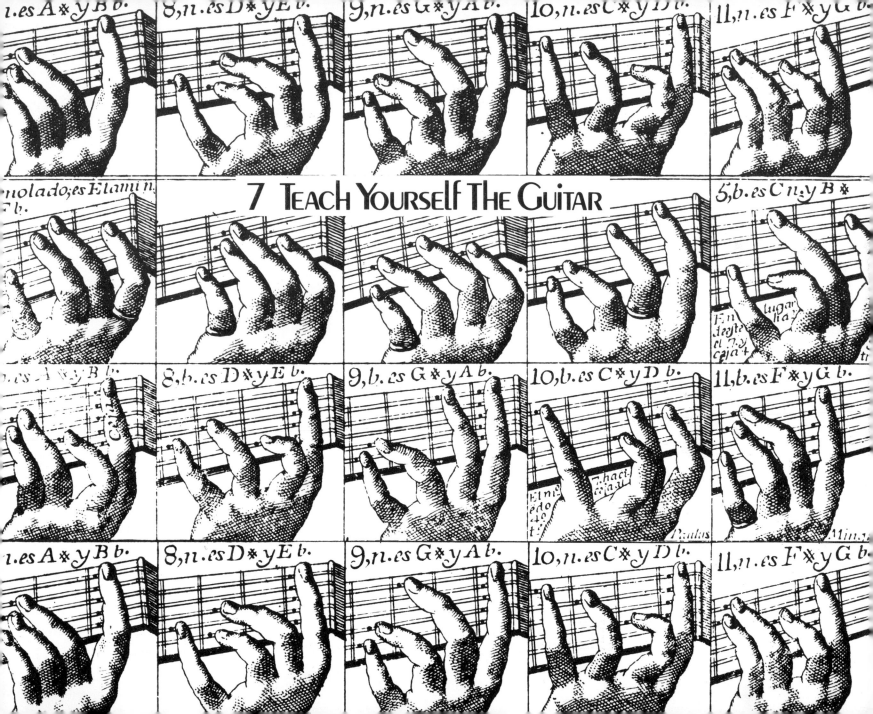

Although it takes a lot of time and patience to learn to play a musical instrument, including the guitar, anyone can 'pick up' a few simple chords quite quickly. This is often just enough to make a simple accompaniment to a song.

An ordinary acoustic guitar (see page 10) is the best instrument to start on. Sit on a straight-backed chair with the guitar resting on your legs crossed as shown in the diagram: you will use your left hand to press the strings down in the correct places, and your right hand to 'strum' the strings. Start by gently strumming the strings without using your left hand to press them down at all, just to get the 'feel' of the instrument. (Fig 1.) If you are left-handed, of course you would strum with your left hand and 'stop' with your right.

Fig 1

Fig 2

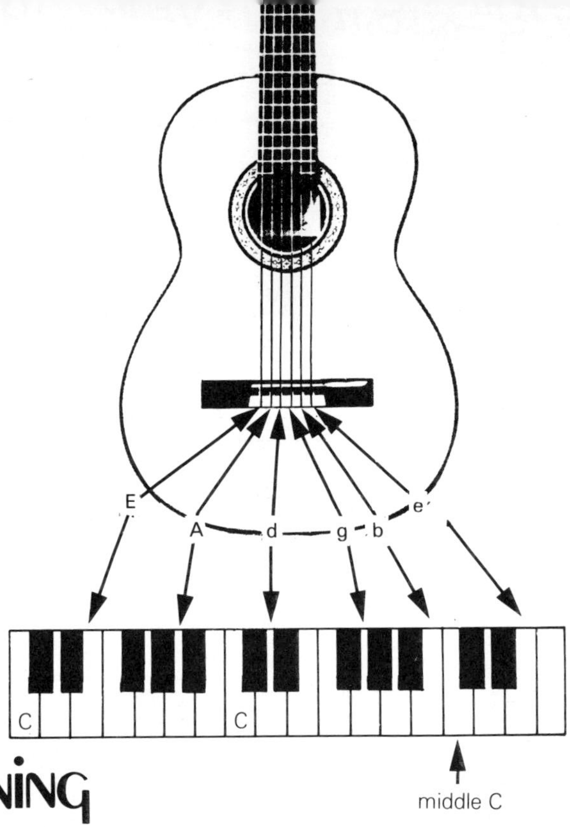

TUNING

If your guitar has been correctly tuned, then the sound you first make by strumming the open strings will sound a little strange. This is because the notes that the strings are usually tuned to do not make up a proper chord.

If your guitar needs tuning (and it probably does if it has not been used for a while), then this could be a little difficult. The reason for this is that you need to be able to hear the correct notes before you can change the strings to match those notes. If you have a piano at home, or a small organ, then tuning will not be difficult—if you don't have a piano then it may be a good idea to ask your music teacher to help you.

The notes that the guitar strings are tuned to are E, A, (two octaves below 'middle c') d, g, b, e. Look at Fig. 2 to see in which order they are tuned.

44

However, since guitar music is *written* an octave higher than it sounds, and the treble clef only is used, the open string notes look like this:

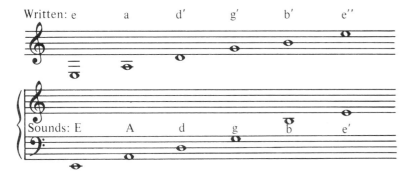

Playing Chords

So that you know which strings to press down when playing a chord and where to press them down, you need to look at Fig. 3, which is an example of a guitar 'window'. All this really is is a picture or diagram of the top three **frets** (see page 4) of the guitar. Wherever there is a circle printed on a string, then that is exactly where you press the string with your fingertips on the guitar: sometimes the fingering will also be shown.

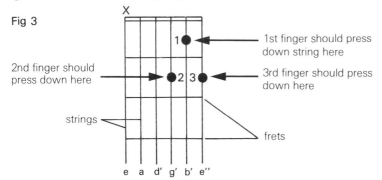

Fig 3

Fig 4

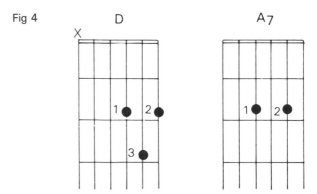

Two chords that are easy to start with are D and A7. The chords shown in Fig. 4 are these, but to make them as easy as possible for you to play you should not play the strings marked with an X. These two chords (D and A7) will enable you to play a number of simple accompaniments to songs like *Oh dear, what can the matter be?* (overleaf). Before you try to play the piece, practise each chord on its own, carefully fingering with the left hand, and strumming with the right: you do this by letting the nails of your fingers brush the strings in a downward movement (see Fig. 5). Once you can do this with each chord, then try changing *slowly* from one chord to the other. When you can do this quite quickly, you are ready to try your first piece!

Other kinds of tuning are sometimes used by folk guitarists, for example **open tuning** (see page 20).

Fig 5

Oh! dear, what can the matter be?

CHORUS

Oh! dear, what can the mat-ter be? Oh! dear, what can the mat-ter be? Oh! dear, what can the mat-ter be?

VERSE

John-ny's so long at the fair._____ He pro-mised to buy me a bas-ket of pos-ies, A gar-land of li-lies, a

gar-land of ros-es. He pro-mised to buy me a bunch of blue rib-bons To tie up my bon-ny brown hair.

He's got the whole world in his hands

More Chords

Some more difficult chords have been printed for you too. These will enable you to play more difficult accompaniments, for example *He's got the whole world in his hands*, which uses the chords of G and D7. Most popular songs have the guitar chords printed on their sheet music, and in songbooks. Your music teacher will also be able to help you find something at just the right level for you to play. You could also try playing the Blues on page 30.

Good luck!

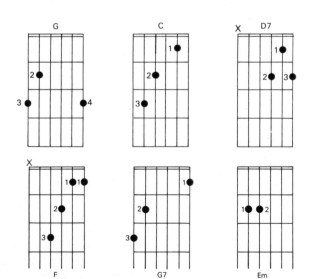

Some Artists' Views Of The Guitar

▲ Greuze: Young man tuning his guitar

▲ Vermeer: The Guitar-player (Kenwood House, London)

▲ Carmontelle: Watercolour (Musee Carnavalet, Paris)

▲ Doré: Engraving of a gipsy guitar-player riding on a donkey

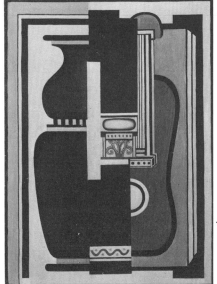

◄ Leger: Blue Guitar and Vase (Kunstmuseum, Basel)

▲ Watteau: *La gamme d'amour* (National Gallery, London)

Books And Records

Records

David Munrow *Instruments of the Middle Ages and Renaissance*
Book: Oxford University Press; Book and Records: EMI SAN
391-2.
Jimi Hendrix Experience *Electric Ladyland* Track Records/Polydor
613 008/9.
John Williams and Sky *Sky 2* Ariola ADSKY 2.
John Williams/English Chamber Orchestra: Rodrigo *Concierto de
Aranjuez* 79334.
John Williams/English Chamber Orchestra: Castelnuovo-Tedesco
Guitar Concerto 79334.
Julian Bream: Villa-Lobos *Five Preludes* RL 43518.

Books

Rex Anderson *Playing the Guitar* Macdonald Guidelines.
Tom and Mary Anne Evans *Guitars* Oxford University Press.